Monarch Butterfly

By Edana Eckart

Welcome Books™

Children's Press®
A Division of Scholastic Inc.
New York / Toronto / London / Auckland / Sydney
Mexico City / New Delhi / Hong Kong
Danbury, Connecticut

Photo Credits: Cover © Siede Preis/Getty Images; pp. 5, 7 © George D. Lepp/Corbis; p. 9 © Nancy Rotenberg/Animals Animals; p. 11 © Richard Cummins/Corbis; pp. 13, 19 © Patti Murray/Animals Animals; p. 15 © Darrell Gulin/Corbis; p. 17 © Breck P. Kent/Animals Animals; p. 21 © Dan Guravich/Corbis
Contributing Editor: Shira Laskin
Book Design: Christopher Logan

Library of Congress Cataloging-in-Publication Data

Eckart, Edana.
    Monarch butterfly / by Edana Eckart.
    p. cm. — (Animals of the world)
    ISBN 0-516-25050-7 (lib. bdg.) — ISBN 0-516-25166-X (pbk.)
    1. Monarch butterfly — Juvenile literature. I. Title.

    QL561.D3E34 2005
    595.78'9—dc22

                                            2004002336

Contents

Monarch butterflies are **insects**.

5

Monarch butterflies are **caterpillars** when they are born.

These caterpillars turn into monarch butterflies.

7

Monarch butterflies have four wings.

Their wings are orange and black with white spots.

9

Monarch butterflies also have six legs.

11

Monarch butterflies live all around the world.

They live in open places, such as **fields**.

13

Monarch butterflies drink **nectar** from flowers.

15

Monarch butterflies lay eggs on **milkweed** plants.

Their eggs are small and white.

17

In the **winter**, many monarch butterflies fly to warm places.

In the **spring**, they fly back home.

Monarch butterflies can fly hundreds of miles.

Monarch butterflies are very beautiful insects.

21

New Words

caterpillars (**kat**-uhr-pil-uhrz) insects that look like short, furry worms with tiny legs and that grow and change into butterflies

fields (**feeldz**) flat, open areas of land without trees or buildings

insects (**in**-sekts) very small animals, such as ants, bees, flies, and mosquitoes, that have three pairs of legs, a pair of antennae on their heads, and sometimes have wings

milkweed (**milk**-weed) a type of plant that monarch butterflies lay their eggs on

monarch butterflies (**mon**-urk **buht**-ur-flyz) large orange-and-black butterflies

nectar (**nek**-tur) a sweet liquid found in many flowers

spring (**spring**) the season between winter and summer, when the weather gets warmer

winter (**wint**-uhr) the season between autumn and spring, when it is cold and snows

22

To Find Out More

Books
Magnificent Monarchs
by Linda Glaser
Millbrook Press

Monarch Butterflies
by Helen Frost
Pebble Books

Web Site
Animal Facts: The Monarch Butterfly
http://www.kidzone.ws/animals/monarch_butterfly.htm
Learn about the monarch butterfly and play games on this Web site.

Index

About the Author
Edana Eckart has written several children's books. She enjoys bike riding with her family.

Reading Consultants
Kris Flynn, Coordinator, Small School District Literacy, The San Diego County Office of Education

Shelly Forys, Certified Reading Recovery Specialist, W.J. Zahnow Elementary School, Waterloo, IL

Paulette Mansell, Certified Reading Recovery Specialist, and Early Literacy Consultant, TX